One Piano, Four Hands—EARLY ADVANCED

EDWARD MacDOWELL

THREE POEMS, Op. 20

Edited by MAURICE HINSON

AF822320

Contents

Keyboard Ensemble Series

Edward MacDowell
(1861–1908)

Prior to the twentieth century, Edward MacDowell was the best-known American composer and was the first to receive international recognition. He began private piano lessons at the age of eight, and at the age of sixteen, MacDowell moved to Paris where he studied the piano privately with Antoine-François Marmontel and composition with Marie-Gabriel Augustin Savard at the Conservatoire. He officially entered the Conservatoire in 1877.

MacDowell later moved to Germany and continued his studies at the Stuttgart Conservatory followed by studies at the Hoch Conservatory in Frankfurt. MacDowell's first concert appearance at the conservatory was on the occasion of a visit on June 9, 1879, by Franz Liszt, in whose honor the students presented a recital of his compositions.

At the end of July 1880 MacDowell left the conservatory and began to teach private piano students. He supplemented his teaching income by accompanying singers and appearing with orchestras. By 1884 four German publishing companies had published ten of his works, including a two-piano version of the First Piano Concerto dedicated to Liszt.

In 1888 MacDowell returned to the United States, where he made his American debut as composer-pianist at a Kneisel Quartet concert at Chickering Hall in Boston. The following year he was invited to perform his new Second Piano Concerto, Op. 23, with the Boston Symphony Orchestra. This was followed by an invitation to perform the concerto in Paris. MacDowell's successes continued. His years in Boston were productive and financially rewarding. He acquired many piano and composition students, gave many concerts, and composed with an intensity that marked the period as the most fruitful of his life. In 1896 he accepted an appointment as Columbia University's first professor of music. He left the University in 1904 but remained in New York, continuing to teach privately.

MacDowell's leading position in American music remained unchallenged for many years. Although he employed the expanded tonal resources of his day, he was not an innovator, and his melodic style remained basically diatonic with occasional touches of chromaticism or modality. His music is largely homophonic. Although his Second Piano Concerto is often performed, he is remembered most for his smaller genre pieces for the piano.

Preface

Edward MacDowell, an outstanding pianist and our greatest nineteenth-century American composer, wrote the **Three Poems, Op. 20,** during the winter months of 1884–1885. These works are character pieces that have a definite poetic basis since all have literary or picturesque titles. They are written in a late-romantic style that uses the evocative power of rich harmonies to respond to the suggestive programmatic titles.

The themes MacDowell used in these pieces are distinguished for their lyricism and nobility. The vitality of their rhythms and the refined and emotionalized harmony are striking. This music shows a fine proportion and symmetry, and each piece maintains a fundamental mood, although striking contrasts are present.

I. *Night by the Sea*
This atmospheric and calm piece shimmers throughout and never rises above a *piano,* dynamically speaking.

II. *A Tale From Knightly Times*
Vigorous and heroic outer sections enclose a lovely, lyrical mid-section. Rhythmic drive coupled with a *marcatissimo* touch is necessary for the robust outer sections.

II. *Ballade*
This short *Allegretto placido* is interlaced with climactic points. The colorful concluding harmonies end the piece and set most effectively.

This edition is dedicated to Dr. J. Bunker Clark and Dr. Jack Winerock, with special admiration and appreciation for their support of American music.

Maurice Hinson

I.
Night by the Sea

Edward MacDowell
edited by Maurice Hinson

Secondo

I.
Night by the Sea

Edward MacDowell
edited by Maurice Hinson

Primo

Secondo

[35]
cre - scen
[40]
dim.
sempre dim.
pp
rall.
con maestà
[45]
tranquillo
[50]
calmato e legatiss.
con 2 Ped.
[55]
ppp
8va
8va

8va
[35]
p
8va
legg.
dim.
sempre dim.
[40]
8va
pp
rall.
[45]
3
[50]
2
calmato e
[55]
legatiss.
8va
ppp

II.
A Tale from Knightly Times

Secondo

Edward MacDowell
edited by Maurice Hinson

Allegro eroico

II.
A Tale from Knightly Times

Edward MacDowell
edited by Maurice Hinson

Primo

[25]
fff marcatiss.
fz
[30]
p
pp
Meno mosso
[35]
pp dolciss.
[40]
fz
ff
cantando
molto marc.
[45]
sempre cresc.
[50]
fz
8va

8va
[25]
fff marcatiss.
martellato
fz
8va
[30]
p
pp
Meno mosso
[35]
p dolciss.
[40]
sempre cresc.
ff
8va
8va
ff
[45]
8va
[50]
marc.
fz

Secondo

[55]
f
p
p
[60]
poco a poco smorz. - - -
[65]
ppp
Tempo I
energico
ppp
sempre cresc.
[70]
fff
pp
[75]
sempre cresc.
[80]
fff
fz
fz
fz
fz

Primo

[55]
f
p
dolce e legatiss.
[60]
[65]
poco a poco smorzando
ppp
Tempo I
energico
pp
[70]
fz
pp
[75]
sempre cresc.
8va
fff
brioso
[80]
8va
marcatiss.
8va
fz

[85]
dolce
[90]
sempre cresc.
p
[95]
cresc.
ff
[100]
fz
marcatiss.
[105]
p
pp
fff

[85]
dolce
8va
[90]
sempre cresc.
p
8va
[95]
ff
8va
[100]
marcatiss.
[105]
p
pp
8va
fff
fz

III.
Ballade

Edward MacDowell
edited by Maurice Hinson

III.
Ballade

Edward MacDowell
edited by Maurice Hinson

Primo

[30]
sempre cresc.
[35]
ff
[40]
marcatiss.
ff non legato
[45]
[50]
fff
poco a
poco dim.
[55]
dolce
[60]
[65]
pp con 2 Ped.
rall.

[30]
sempre cresc.
[35]
ff
[40]
marcatiss.
8va
8va
[45]
fff
[50]
poco a poco dim.
[55]
dolce
[60]
sempre dim.
pp
3

[70]
dolce
[75]
[80]
non legato
cresc.
[85]
fff maestoso
[90]
marc. poco a poco
[95]
dim.
[100]
p
dolce
sempre
[105]
dim.
smorz.
rall.
ppp
ppp

8va
[70]
[75]
p placido
dolente
8va
[80]
fff
fff
marcatiss.
8va
[85]
fff maestoso
8va
[90]
[95]
8va
[100]
p
dolce
sempre dim.
[105]
smorz.
rall.
ppp